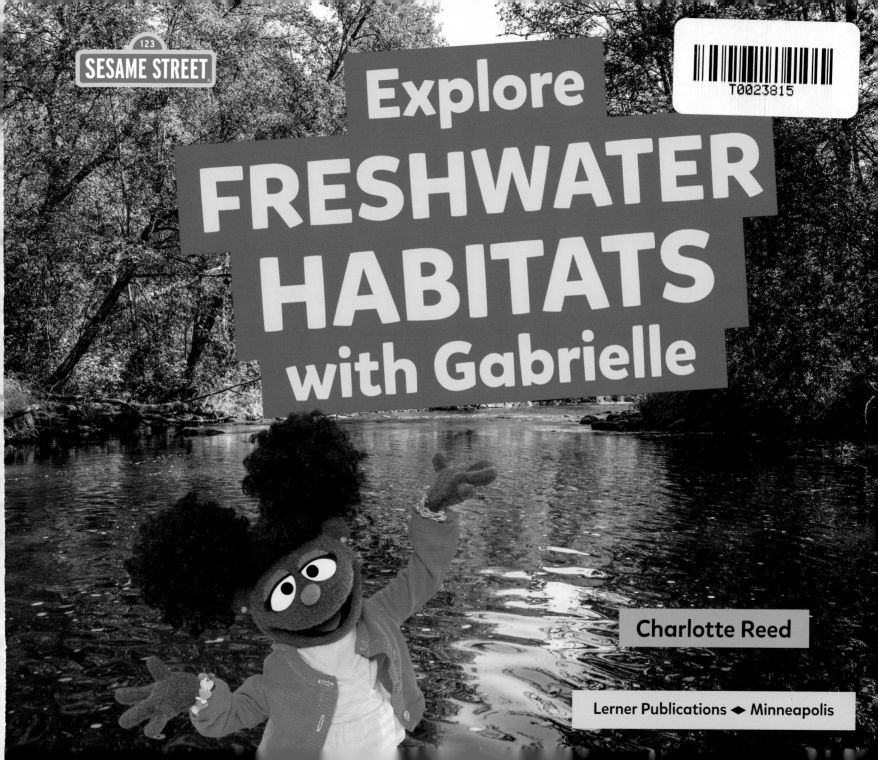

SESAME STREET

Explore
FRESHWATER HABITATS
with Gabrielle

Charlotte Reed

Lerner Publications ◆ Minneapolis

There are many habitats to explore!

In the Sesame Street® Habitats series, young readers will take a tour of eight habitats. Join your friends from *Sesame Street* as they learn about these different habitats where animals live, sleep, and find food and water.

Sincerely,
The Editors at Sesame Workshop

Table of Contents

WHAT IS A HABITAT?

Let's explore habitats! A habitat is a place where animals live, sleep, and find food and water. A freshwater habitat is a type of habitat.

There are many kinds of freshwater habitats!

Rivers, creeks, ponds, lakes, and some swamps are examples of freshwater habitats.

Streams are another freshwater habitat!

LET'S LOOK AT FRESHWATER HABITATS

Freshwater habitats are home to many different types of animals and plants. Lots of fish live in freshwater habitats.

Turtles live in freshwater habitats too!

This catfish lives at the bottom of a river. Catfish have barbels around their mouth. Barbels help catfish smell and taste food.

Barbels look like a cat's whiskers! That's how catfish got their name.

Alligators live on the surface of some swamps. Their nose is on top of their head so they can breathe while swimming.

Alligators are great swimmers!

Water lilies grow in lakes and ponds. They have flowers and leaves that float on the surface of the water. These leaves are called lily pads.

Frogs sometimes sit on top of a lily pad!

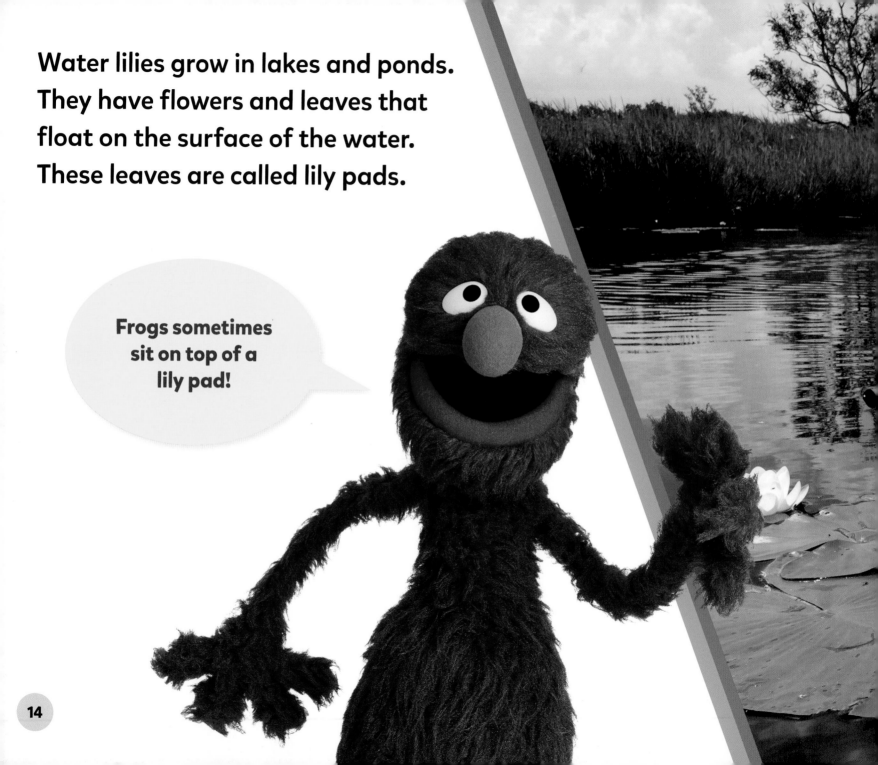

Cattail plants grow in fresh water.
Their roots help keep the water clean.
Some birds, like the blackbird, build
their nests in them!

A nest is where a
bird lays its eggs.

Newts live on land and in ponds, creeks, and lakes. They have four legs to walk on land, and a long, flat tail to swim in the water.

Newt babies are sometimes called newt tadpoles.

Many ducks live in freshwater habitats. Ducks have waterproof feathers that help them keep warm in the water, on land, or in the air.

Elmo likes to snuggle in a blanket to keep warm!

21

Some freshwater habitats have a wall made of sticks and mud. This is called a dam. Dams are made by beavers.

Beavers build lodges out of sticks and mud.

A lodge is a beaver's home!

River otters mostly live in rivers, streams, lakes, and ponds. Their homes are called dens.

Me home is on Sesame Street!

Freshwater habitats are home to all these plants and animals, and more!

I love learning about freshwater habitats!

CAN YOU GUESS?

1. Which of these pictures is of a freshwater habitat?

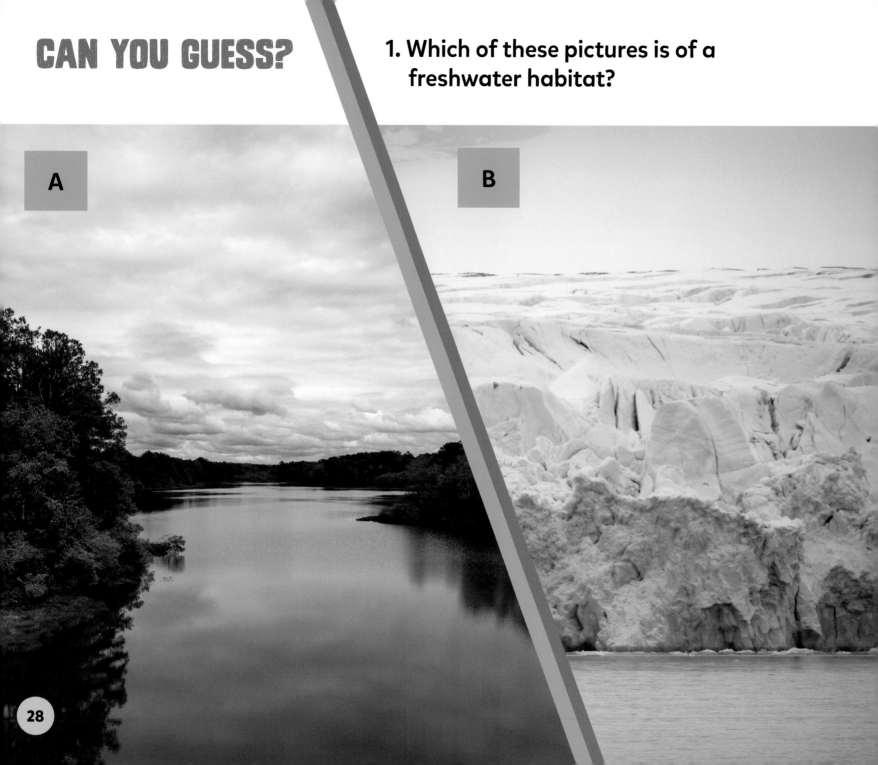

A

B

2. Which of these animals lives in a freshwater habitat?

A

B

Glossary

barbels: a part of the fish that looks like whiskers

dam: a structure like a wall that holds back water

habitat: a place where animals live and can find water, food, and a place to sleep

roots: parts of plants that are usually underground

Can You Guess? Answers
1. A
2. B

Read More

Andrus, Aubre. *In the Pond*. Washington, DC: National Geographic Kids, 2022.

Nargi, Lela. *Freshwater Biomes*. Minneapolis: Jump!, 2023.

Reed, Charlotte. *Explore Rain Forest Habitats with Abby*. Minneapolis: Lerner Publications, 2024.

Photo Acknowledgments

Martins Vanags/Getty Images, p. 1; skibreck/Getty Images, p. 5; MilanMaksovic/Getty Images, p. 6; Elenakirey/Getty Images, p. 9; mirecca/Getty Images, p. 10; Vladimir Wrangel/Shutterstock, p. 11; Mark Newman/Getty Images, p. 13; Sjo/Getty Images, p. 15; kj2011/Getty Images, p. 15 (Frog); Peter Blottman Photography/Getty Images, p. 17 (Blackbird); malven57/Getty Images, p. 17 (Cattails); CreativeNature_nl/Getty Images, p. 18; Douglas Rissing/Getty Images, p. 19; taviphoto/Getty Images, p. 20; DeniseBush/Getty Images, p. 22; Jillian Cooper/Getty Images, p. 22 (Beaver); kavunchik/Getty Images, p. 24; Hogo/Getty Images, p. 25; Wirestock/Getty Images, p. 26 (Blackbird); SERHII LUZHEVSKYI/Getty Images, p. 26 (Ducks); Robitaille/Getty Images, p. 26-27 (Turtle); BrianLasenby/Getty Images, p. 27 (Otters); George Dodd/Getty Images, p. 28 (Left); Brett Monroe Garner/Getty Images, p. 28 (Right); Christina Radcliffe/Getty Images, p. 29 (Beaver); twildlife/Getty Images, p. 29 (Mountain goat).
Cover: Jillian Cooper/Getty Images, (Beaver); Gabberr/Getty Images, (Frog); Fyletto/Getty Images, (Pond); Nat Photos/Getty Images, (Water lilies).

Index

For the little girl who loved animals and writing stories. Look at us now!

Lerner Publications Company
An imprint of Lerner Publishing Group, Inc.
241 First Avenue North
Minneapolis, MN 55401 USA

For reading levels and more information, look up this title at www.lernerbooks.com.

Main body text set in Mikado provided by HVD.

Editor: Amber Ross **Designer:** Laura Otto Rinne

Library of Congress Cataloging-in-Publication Data

Names: Reed, Charlotte, 1997- author.
Title: Explore freshwater habitats with Gabrielle / Charlotte Reed.
Description: Minneapolis : Lerner Publications, [2024] | Series: Sesame Street habitats | Includes bibliographical references and index. | Audience: Ages 4-8 | Audience: Grades K-1 | Summary: "Rivers, creeks, ponds, swamps, and lakes are all freshwater habitats. Join Gabrielle and her Sesame Street friends as they explore the plants and animals of freshwater habitats"– Provided by publisher.
Identifiers: LCCN 2023004543 (print) | LCCN 2023004544 (ebook) | ISBN 9798765604274 (library binding) | ISBN 9798765617502 (epub)
Subjects: LCSH: Freshwater animals–Habitations–Juvenile literature. | Freshwater ecology–Juvenile literature. | BISAC: JUVENILE NONFICTION / Science & Nature / Environmental Science & Ecosystems
Classification: LCC QL141 .R435 2024 (print) | LCC QL141 (ebook) | DDC 591.76–dc23/eng/20230503

LC record available at https://lccn.loc.gov/2023004543
LC ebook record available at https://lccn.loc.gov/2023004544

ISBN 979-8-7656-2485-2 (pbk.)

Manufactured in the United States of America
1-1009564-51414-6/2/2023